Tuesday's Muse 2

More fuel for the fire and passion of your life.

Also by J. Todd Jenkins:

Tuesday's Muse
(Visual and Verbal Appetizers for the Great Banquet of Your Life)
2013
ISBN: 9781484980521

Tuesday's Muse 2
(More Fuel for the Fire and Passion of Your Life)
Copyright 2015
J. Todd Jenkins
All rights reserved.
ISBN: 1507860765

Contents

Acknowledgments

This project would never have been completed without the help and encouragement, editorial comments, layout suggestions, and proofreading of Joanie Lukins and Carie Turner. I also could not have finished this collection without the wonderful cover design by Susan Moore Graham, and the powerful photographic contributions of friends and relatives: Cyndi Crafton Bagley, Kathy Chambers, Kendall Cox, Jane Hines, Jennie Roberts Jenkins, Owen Todd Jenkins, Katie Jenkins Kester, Lee Lindsey McKinney, Keith Powell, Anne Shurley, and Holly Jenkins Williams. I am especially grateful for the many people who encouraged me to use color photographs in this second volume.

Introduction

Tuesday's Muse 2 is a fragrant blend of pastoral prayers, prophetic calls, and hopeful imaginings birthed from immersion in a struggle with the particularity of life and faith. Over the past decade, I've heard many religious people call for "Prayer Warriors" in the midst of one crisis or another. Once, when I received such a particular call via email, I responded with, "Is there room for Prayer Poets also?" That eventually led me to:

Fireweed

Prayer Warriors abound,
but for Prayer Poets we plead.
Death's stench is all around;
showers of silence we need.

> Give us the space at the table
> for old words to be re-shaped
> into new shelters capable

> of storying unimaginable horror
> into not only breath for today,

> but hope for tomorrow.

Poetry and prayer have a number of things in common. Both push language to its limits in an attempt to describe the expanse of the human condition, as well as articulate our earthly perspective on the divine-human interface. They are equal respecters of blank space and silence, because these are the places where others are invited to join the conversation – both the "other" of God and the "other" of neighbor. *Tuesday's Muse 2* is an invitation for readers to join their own stories with those of the community of faith.

Habakkuk 2:19
Alas for you who
say to the wood,
"Wake up!" to
silent stone,
"Rouse yourself!"
Can it teach? See,
it is gold and silver
plated, and there
is no breath in it at
all.
20 But the Lord is
in his holy temple;
let all the earth
keep silence
before him!

(Photo by Lee Lindsey McKinney)

Prayer Poet

The psalmists knew very well
how carefully loaded phrases
strung together in surprising ways
can be explosive in both
hopeful and dangerous ways;

how hurling guttural truth
toward the heavens changes
the world in ways we can
neither explain nor predict;

how leaving wide margins
of blank silence leaves room
for the other voice to speak.

The pieces that both come from
and travel to the deepest places
often begin with empty lines,

which represent the ways
we duct-tape the voices in our head
long enough to hear the one in our heart.

Those are the ones asking us
questions which most need answering;
questions that all creation asks daily;
questions that weave us into
a tapestry of history and hope.

Psalm 73:26
My flesh and my
heart
may fail,
but God is the
strength of my heart
and my portion
forever.

This Train

This train didn't ask if you wanted to go;
didn't send you an enticing brochure;
didn't try to convince you that going
would be the trip of a lifetime.

    This train snatched you up
    in the middle of the night,
    in the middle of your life,
    in the middle of your plans and dreams.

        This train's conductor doesn't seem to care
        if you have a ticket or not,
        if you pull the stop-cord continuously,
        if you protest with voice and/or violence.

            This train's passengers may not know you,
            may not seem to acknowledge your presence,
            may not want to hear your story because
            their own stories are playing so loudly.

This train won't divulge your destination,
won't tell you how long it will take
or where you may stop along the way
or what it will be like when you arrive.

This train's conductor may lead you to believe
that this is a trip that must be done solo,
that no one else would dare join you,
that no one else knows how to board.

This train's conductor doesn't know
things and people that you know,
doesn't know that while others are not wholly able
to ride in your seat or one like it,

they are still with you, lining the track at every curve,
steadying the car with calming prayers,
nourishing peace with casseroles of love,
smoothing the tracks with tears of passion.

This train's conductor has long-forgotten
the conductor-of-all-conductors who
put the only son on the life-train once
and opened a new rail-line after three days.

This train now follows these new tracks
and though we are not privy to what lies ahead,
our faith is anchored in the conductor-of-all-conductors,
our journey and destination secured by this resurrection rail-line.

Isaiah 9: 2 The people who walked in darkness
have seen a great light;
those who lived in a land of deep darkness —
on them
light
has shined.

(Photo by Anne Shurley)

Spending

Advent's call to wait, watch, prepare
didn't outlast Thanksgiving's leftover turkey;
"O Come, O Come Emmanuel" gave way
to "O Little Town of Bethlehem."

The family candle ritual fell
as the calendar filled with fun;
the bell lap comes earlier each year,
pushing, pressing; fibrillation nears.

The devotional book gathers dust
as cable inundates us with new classics.
How many twists and technologies can we find
to complicate and reintroduce Nicholas' gift?

Worship at the cathedral of the mall
intensifies as credit tachometers
whine beyond the red zone;
package toting enhances subluxation.

Always one step ahead of where we are;
spirit, mind, body—
never the three shall meet;
standing in line, expecting only to
exchange presents instead of presence.

Beyond the mall manger's baby powder scent
the Christ child begs our attention;
the true spending gift of Christmas
is risking honest time sharing love.

Psalm 50:1 The mighty one, God the Lord,
speaks and summons the earth
from the rising of the sun to its setting.

(Photo by Lee Lindsey McKinney)

Winter Sunset

As struggle/transition
(synonymous most often)
between day and night
neared its inevitable conclusion –

  just when I thought the sun
  would acquiesce painlessly –
  she opened a vein,
  letting flow a crimson river.

  Clouds, tipping their hand,
  soaked up the blood like nurses
  gently gauzing surgical incision,
  evidencing their complicity in the coup.

    Of course, dark eventually triumphed,
    but through sun's epic struggle,
    those of us facing night's rage
    remember her promised return;
    winter's pall is not quite so ominous.

      This daily sacrifice,
      played out on every horizon,
      with infinite variety,
      shores-up fragile walls of faith,
      reminds us: grace and God
      are as ever-tenacious
      in pursuit of our future.

        Thanks be to edge of earth and sky!

2 Prayers for Worship

(Photo by Jane Hines)   **Invocation**

God of open invitation beyond our ability to comprehend, we do not mean to come to worship with so many expectations of control and so little anticipation of surprise; but it is sometimes hard for us to trust that you have a plan for us. When we feel helpless, remind us that we never really were in control. When we feel lost, insignificant, and hopeless, remind us that you have found us, you have declared us to be of great value, and you love us. If we are capable of invoking anything this morning, O Lord, let it be our willingness to accept your gracious invitation to let your will unfold its hope and promise into all of the places where we are broken open; through Jesus Christ, our Lord. Amen.

Illumination

When we close our eyes, O God, the light, no matter its source, becomes nearly invisible to us. We might as well be in a deep cave whose twisting tunnels have blocked every lumen. Is that why this is such a good posture for prayer? Do we close our eyes so that all of the glorious visual stimuli of creation won't distract us from the light that you've put in our hearts?

Give us courage, this day and every day, to step toward the shadows of life, to struggle with the stories that connect us to you and one another, and to do so as those whose faith mortars the vast expanse between our tiny bricks of understanding; through Jesus Christ our Lord. Amen.

Romans 15: 13
May the
God of hope
fill you with all
joy and peace
in believing,
so that you may
abound in hope
by the power of the
Holy Spirit.

Showing Up

Singing in the face
of evil, chaos, and uncertainty
is what defines faith.

Not just singing
any old tune or lyrics;
but belting out melodies
that hauntingly dare us
to step toward the darkness,

and lyrics which proclaim,
in spite of the appearance
of current circumstances,
that fear, anxiety, hatred, scarcity
are not gaining momentum.

They are, instead, screaming vestiges
of evil who already know
that love has won.

Sing on, sisters and brothers;
the world is dying to claim
the courage of this opus,

where new is not replacement
but resurrection to something
we've yet the wherewithal to imagine.

Joel 1:3 Tell your children of it, and let your children tell their children, and their children another generation.

(Photo by Keith Powell)

Passing Witnesses

Not the rubber-neckers of Interstate infamy,
slowing down to gawk at the scene,
nearly causing a wreck themselves,
just for an opportunity to eavesdrop
on the tragedy of another.

Instead, those whose station and age
place them at the sacred intersection
where one generation's path joins
the communion of the saints in light.

May they be upheld by strong arms
as they serve as involuntary acolytes,
transmitting life's flickering flame
from the generation in front
to the one that trails behind.

Undergird them with tender hands
as the baton is passed through them;
stories, faith, lessons contained
in what they've heard, seen, learned.

Tinge their reverence with levity,
their respect with humor,
that grief may not overcome,
sorrow may not swallow,
silence may not overwhelm.

"Your grandmother used to say…"
"I remember the time my grandfather…"
May these words be used just enough
to safely guide tomorrow's travelers.

2 Kings 4:10 Let us make a small roof chamber with walls, and put there for him a bed, a table, a chair, and a lamp, so that he can stay there whenever he comes to us."

Christmas Eve

You know the day is bound to be long
when it's called an "eve" at sunrise.
Long it is for many folks in varied ways.

Long for those whose hopes are set
on simple magic of chimneys, sleigh,
airborne reindeer, gifts galore.

Long for those whose plans are such
to stave off disappointment from
such childlike dreams of abundance;

working and saving for eleven months;
decorating and preparing for weeks;
outlasting excitement to assemble.

Long for those little ones whose hopes
are beaten down 24/7 by birth, circumstance
but can't help hoping one more time.

Longer still for beleaguered parents from
the have-not side of life who
must figure out
how to explain tomorrow's emptiness.

Longing is a deeper long for
those whose pain
is heightened by the absence
of a life-long love
or knowledge that this year
may be the last.

Into this long and longing day that
moves toward darkness all too soon,
a candle flicker moves toward life.

For those whose patience births a faith,
nurturing a flame that warms a hope,
single candle turns to tongues of fire.

Light, warmth, grace all overflow;
gold, frankincense, myrrh arrive;
joy is stirred deep in the soul!

Genesis 28:12 And he dreamed
that there was a ladder set up on the earth,
the top of it reaching to heaven;
and the angels of God were
ascending and descending on it.

Mission's Meal

As cultures, economies, faiths,
and people's lives intertwine
in this ever-shrinking world,
inequity of circumstances and resources
inevitably weaves a fragile tapestry.

Warp threads extend vertically,
from earth to heaven,
stretching to connect
creation and holy hope;
declaring independence and worth.

Woof threads span horizontally,
from person to person, life to life,
drawing us together as family,
posing questions of abundance, scarcity,
exposing interdependence as two-way street.

Respect is invited to the table
as stories, faith, lives are shared,
understanding supplants judgment,
trust trumps angst and fear,
all hunger for God's sustenance.

Dignity becomes a possibility
when resources are controlled
by those who have a need;
we/they becomes us,
stuff becomes God's.

Sustainability must be addressed
from both directions simultaneously,
mine and yours, ours and theirs.
How can we both live and serve
with what we have and haven't?

Tapestry of mission and service
unfurls into intended form
when we all allow ourselves
to be fed by the long-handled spoon
of one another's gifts and grace.

Psalm 59:17 O my strength,
I will sing praises to you,
for you, O God, are my fortress,
the God who shows me steadfast love.

Stormy Blast

"O God, our help in ages past,
our hope for years to come,
our shelter from the stormy blast
and our eternal home."

If e'r there were an icy blast,
the news today is one.
Send shelter now to hold us fast:
the warmth of your dear Son.

Life as we thought we knew it was,
has changed beyond our fears.
Chaos seems to reign because
we face fast-ending years.

Life's river often runs so deep;
its currents are too strong.
Provide an oar of faith to keep
so we may sing your song.

Give us the strength to face the end
with hope and courage true.
As we return where we begin
we find our grace in you.

Buttons

Lord, you know that family knows best
how and when to push my buttons.
They seem to do it most often when
I am already teetering on the edge.

Plink, click, and before I know it,
I'm dangerously down the road to destruction,
being jet-propelled by a volatile mix
of unexamined emotions-on-steroids.

By the time I regain my senses,
our path is littered with the debris
of the verbal and emotional carnage
whose execution I can scarcely recall.

Perhaps I could fashion a cover
keeping the buttons safe from touch;
"Deal or No Deal" strong, so that
not even those who know could succeed.

Or maybe with my tears I could
rust and corrode their mechanism
so at least they would be harder to push,
giving me advanced, def-con warning.

The little voice inside tells me
that the blame lies with the pusher
and not so much the pushee
but I really know better.

Give me the courage to do
a little gardening of the soul;
to dig up the humus of my life
accepting myself for who I am;

to decompose the hurt and grief
long-buried, but never acknowledged;
giving grace a chance to work its mystery
turning forgiveness deeply
into the compost-pile.

(Photo by Jennie Roberts Jenkins)

Call to Worship

[one] *We're probably here because the people who were here before us gave birth to us, married us, worked with us, befriended us, or invited us.*

[many] **We're also here because God put a longing deep inside us that has not yet been satisfied.**

[one] *We've tried to satisfy this longing – this hunger – with many other things:*

[many] **material possessions, food, superficial relationships, busy schedules, and more.**

[one] *Could this be a day when we find more of the answers for how to fill the emptiness and dissatisfaction?*

[many] **That's what we're hoping. That's why we came.**

[all] ***Let us open wide, dig deep, and dare to let God loose!***

2 Samuel 9:6 Mephibosheth son of Jonathan son of Saul came to David, and fell on his face and did obeisance. David said, "Mephibosheth!" He answered, "I am your servant." 7 David said to him, "Do not be afraid, for I will show you kindness for the sake of your father Jonathan; I will restore to you all the land of your grandfather Saul, and you yourself shall eat at my table always."

Dinner Bell

When eye cannot see beyond I,
self loses sight of the other;
the world is a dark, cold place,
we're orphaned from sister and brother.

Consumption becomes the main function,
surrounded by layers of our stuff;
life's an ultimate competition,
everything is never enough.

Construction becomes our destruction:
wall, door, lock, fence, gate;
neighbor becomes adversary,
survival is fueled by hate.

As if Exodus had nothing to do with us,
we cling to our titles and deeds,
claiming earth as our own creation.
I'm the flower; you are the weeds.

Freedom to travel begins to unravel
as home becomes the place
where liberty's armed to the teeth
and all have forgotten grace.

Are we unable to come to the table,
where wine is poured and bread broken,
where prodigal and steadfast alike,
find love both lived and spoken?

Genesis 2:7 ...then the Lord God
formed man from the dust of the
ground, and breathed into his
nostrils the breath of life;
and the man became
a living being.

Life and Death

In times like these, O Lord,
  we are not sure whether we are
   living at the speed of death, or
    dying at the speed of life, or
      whether there is a whit of difference
       between the paradox of these two phrases.

As age progresses, life is taken
  away from us, ever so slowly, so
    that we hardly notice it at all.
      But disease comes along and speeds
        up the process: a foot here, a kidney there,
          crumbling joints and failing organs all around.

Then death sneaks up and snatches!
      Our breath is taken away all at once.

Give us, O Lord, our breath back;
        help us to breathe your spirit once more.
            Help us to remember that life isn't
              merely bodily function; meaning is
                not given by heart beat or brain wave.

Give us, O Lord, your mysterious
        gift of memory that we may
            grasp the spark of divine grace that
              showed through the one we hold dear;
              bless us with the riches of remembrance and
                  the fame of love; through the remembered One.

Luke 11:4 (KJV) And forgive us our sins;
for we also forgive every one
that is indebted to us.
And lead us not into temptation;
but deliver us from evil.

Independence Deliverance

Deliver us, O Lord, from politicians
who would abuse Old Glory
by hiding behind her as if
she were an illusionist's curtain,
waving her red and blue before us,
clouding our eyes with the mists
of mystery, respect, and history,
as all manner of self-promotion and sell-outs
are carried on behind her cloister.

> Protect us, O God, from corporations
> who would misuse the stars and stripes
> by cloaking their products in her sacredness,
> using her beauty as slight-of-hand distraction,
> while gouging our hearts, minds, and bodies
> with misrepresented, self-interested greed
> that will one day cost us our souls.

> Keep back from us, El Shaddai, religious institutions
> and their unscrupulous champions
> who would confuse the beauty and mirth
> of democracy's freedom which she represents,
> with your salvific Word-become-flesh,
> who demands that even nations submit
> to the critique of your healing flame of holiness.

Leviticus 25:10 And you shall hallow the fiftieth year and you shall proclaim liberty throughout the land to all its inhabitants. It shall be a jubilee
for you: you shall return, every one of you, to your property and every one of you to your family.

Duplicity

Give me your tomatoes,
your peppers, your hybrid melons,
yearning to be consumed,
but not so much your tired,
your poor, your huddled masses
yearning to breathe free.

The wretched refuse of bowing
to chemicals and corporations
has our shores teeming with toxicity,
and our hearts quivering with xenophobia.

The tempest-tossed who dream
of hope will not so much be met
 with lamp at golden door
as laser sight and incarceration.

All the while, our consumptive greed
turns a blind eye to the duplicity
of deportation and the rending
of family's fabric, to which
we claim undying allegiance.

Who will resurrect liberty?

"Give me your tired, your poor,
Your huddled masses yearning to breathe free,
The wretched refuse of your teeming shore.
Send these, the homeless, tempest-tossed, to me:
I lift my lamp beside the golden door."
— Emma Lazarus

*Exodus 3:7 Then the Lord said,
"I have observed the misery
of my people who are in Egypt;
I have heard their cry
on account of their
taskmasters.
Indeed, I know their sufferings,
8 and I have come down
to deliver them from the
Egyptians,
and to bring them up out
of that land to
a good and broad land,
a land flowing with
milk and honey...*

Hope's Seed

When all that we hope for has been
    snatched from underneath us,
        we come face to face with
            the seed and root of hope itself:

the eternal presence and promise
    of grace. Our deepest gratitude
        for this gift is expressed in the courage
            and compassion to risk uncensored presence
                in the midst of another's attempt at dying well;

        or even to endure the pain
            of helplessly watching someone's
                unnecessarily horrible death because
                    their image of self could not be rescued
                        from the prison of its own Hell.

            Prayers for all of us whose living
                will enter the grave with the dead.
                    May their love greet us on the far side
                        of this deep and shadowed valley,
                            pulling us, by faith, deeper
                                into life's joy and meaning.

Genesis 45: 15 And he kissed all his brothers
and wept upon them; and after that
his brothers talked with him.

Grace Is the Word
Bicentennial hymn for First Presbyterian Church
Fayetteville, Tennessee 2012
(Sung to St. Anne CM)

Before bricks on this corner stood
to form a worship space,
God was at work perfecting good,
in every time and place.

We now lift up our joyous praise
for opportunity
to serve in love beyond our days
through this community.

O God, you help throughout our days;
you guide the strong and weak.
Show us the wisdom of your ways
as we your mission seek.

Grace is the word that's spoken here;
we seek to let it flow
as hope and comfort far and near
so everyone will know!

Genesis 41:43 He had him ride
in the chariot of his second-in-command;
and they cried out in front of him,
"Bow the knee!"
Thus he set him over all the land of Egypt.

Idol

The ancients fashioned images
of various animals, both real life
and in combinations
outside the realm of genetic possibility,
to augment and direct their worship.

Judaism, Christianity, and Islam
eschew such visual representations,
proclaiming that the full self
of the one true God
cannot be visually observed
in two or three dimensions.

But do not fool yourself
into believing that we have thus
avoided practicing idolatry.

Wherever there is a rule
or topic whose examination
is beyond the reach of faith,

whenever a conversation has been
excluded from our shared sacred story,
you can rest assured that Baal
is just as present as ever.

That which we dare not discuss
is the very thing toward which
our lives instinctively genuflect.

*Matthew 7:2 For with the judgment
you make you will be judged,
and the measure you give
will be the measure you get.*

Measure of Grace

How do we determine what we will value?
By envy's green reflected in the eyes
of others as well as in the mirror, or
by the longings of our heart?

(Photo by Kathy Chambers)

How do we measure what we value?
Let me count the ways:
appearance, uniformity, popularity,
expectation, cost, comparison.

Then there comes the day
when unimaginable gift appears;
gift of unexpected proportions;
of unexplained mystery.

Then all desires that once burned,
all quantifications that loomed large,
suddenly recede into insignificance
and we are left breathless by sheer surprise.

Loving for the sake of love;
giving because we can do no other;
letting go to become everything
and nothing more than exactly
what God created us to be.

When our connectedness sinks in
and relationship becomes our identity,
all the former things will pass away;
we will finally know the measure of grace.

*Luke 2:15 And it came to pass, as the angels were gone away from them into heaven,
the shepherds said one to another,
Let us now go even unto Bethlehem, and
see this thing
which is come to pass,
which the Lord hath made known unto us. 16 And they came with haste,
and found Mary, and Joseph, and the babe lying in a manger.*

Imagine

It's December 26, of all days,
and the very self of God has decided
to visit creation again, *en carne*.

> Forget, for a moment, if you can,
> what this time will look like to us;
> try to picture what it will look like to God.

> In much of the world, it will be
> just another day of need:
> toil and suffering
> in the struggle to survive.

> Perhaps the remains
> of a meager celebration
> from the night before
> might be visible
> to the trained eye:

a candle and the crumbs
from a small portion
of seldom-splurged-for food.

And then there's my neck of the woods:
cardboard boxes, brightly colored paper,
ribbon, partially-eaten animal carcasses
and every food imaginable heaped at the curb
as if an omnivore named opulence
has binged and purged on the spot;

     people scurrying to hide every vestige
     of what's not discarded from the extravaganza
     in attics, garages, and storage buildings for another year
     before returning to the security of their compounds.

          Where will this generation's shepherds be found –
          those at the margins whose work
          is both so menial and odoriferous
          that they must be kept at bay?

               What will be their response
               to the celestial's visit and proclamation:
               "Glory to God in the highest heaven,
                and on earth peace among those whom he favors!"?

     When they arrive in our neighborhood,
     will we recognize them as the favored ones?
     Will we join Mary in treasuring
     their words in our hearts?

Or will their uniforms and smelly trucks
cause our eyes and hearts to glaze?
If you were playing this like the stock market,
how heavily would you leverage
your portfolio for the future they're promising?

Luke 16:19 "There was a rich man who was dressed in purple and fine linen and who feasted sumptuously every day. 20 And at his gate lay a poor man named
Lazarus,
covered with sores,
21 who longed to satisfy his hunger with what fell from the rich man's table; even the
dogs
would come and lick his sores.

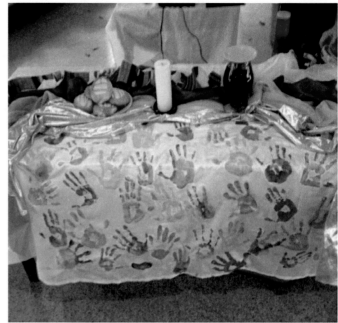

Sumptuous

I'm sure I never looked finer today,
rolling into church in my purple shirt,
fresh off a Saturday evening
of sumptuous grilled chicken, rich onion pie,
and flavorful bacon ranch potato salad,
along with the beverage of my choice.

And then I had to listen to Jesus
get all-up-in the Pharisees' face
about a rich guy, whose name we'll never know,
and an oozing-scabbed beggar
at his gate whose name means "God is with me."

"It's a good thing I'm not rich!"
I thought, as I measured myself
against Forbes' list.

That's when I noticed God's gaze.
It was a lot broader, and maybe
even deeper, than mine.

I was looking at Gates, and God
was looking at Guatemala and Ghana.
I was seeing Buffet, and God
was seeing Belize and Botswana.

I was imaging the Kochs, and God
could clearly see Kenya and Kandahar.
I was looking up at the "Haves", and God
was looking over at Honduras and Haiti.

Lazarus: "We are not alone."
So when we feel estranged,
isolated, gated, and afraid,
perhaps it is a loss of central vision –

a failure to recognize our *raison d'être* –
and a focus on the peripheral.
Perhaps it is time to get back
to the heart of the matter;
back to the table where all are welcome.

24

Acts 21: 5 When our days there were ended,
we left and proceeded on our journey;
and all of them, with wives and children,
escorted us outside the city.
There we knelt down on the beach and prayed...

Graduated

Another chapter in the books.
Never can we return to this place.
Remember this time, this feel, these looks;
moving forward in time and space.

Tomorrow's chapter awaits its writing;
dreams, hopes, and possibility.
Adjust the seat, mirrors, lighting;
future emerges from focus, ability.

Start each day with passion's fire;
lessons to learn, skills to master.
Eagles' wings soar higher and higher;
days coming at you, faster and faster.

Backward glancing one day, we'll celebrate;
youth's enthusiasm evokes joyful tears.
Future's ours, and it won't wait;
unfolding gift of all our years.

Psalm 85:10
Steadfast love
and faithfulness
will meet;
righteousness and peace
will kiss each other.

Rock, Paper, Scissors

> Three ways to have it all,
> or so it seems;
> each in its own right
> a recipe for domination.

> Smash it all to hell
> with a heavy blow,
> knocking the breath
> out of your neighbor so that
> your way is the only way.

> Wrap it all in a giant blanket,
> not from grandma's quilt collection,
> but a thinly pressed piece
> of processed pulp,
> producing agonizing asphyxia,
> or at least blindness.

> Divide and conquer;
> slice and dice all opposition
> into easily dismissed
> slivers of meaninglessness.

What do you do with the fool,
holy as she is, who dares
to play a fourth option;
one that flies below the radar
of conventional warfare: *heart*?

*Matthew 6:19 "Do not store up
for yourselves treasures on earth,
where moth and rust consume
and where thieves break in and steal;*

Heart for It

When Jesus says,
*"For where your treasure is,
there your heart will be also." (Matthew 6:21)*
he's not saying that our treasure
will follow our heart.

He knows that whatever we value,
our hearts will find their way to it.
Whatever we don't value,
our hearts will not seek out.

If economics is our driving force –
if we determine both God's love for us
and therefore our love for others
by the number of baskets
of leftovers we can collect;

if time is short and we schedule
and protect all of ours
for fear that there won't be enough
for us to enjoy the fruits of your bounty
(or "our labor" as we are wont to call it) –

then, when a matter of mission
or justice or compassion
comes our way and we say,
"We don't have the time or money for it."
what we are really saying is,
"We don't have the heart for it."

Give us hearts for it, O God!

Song of Solomon 2:10 My beloved
speaks and says to me:
"Arise, my love, my fair one, and
come away;
11 for now the winter is past, the
rain is over and gone.

Love
(by Holly Jenkins Williams)

When you love, you
sow resilient little seeds
deeply into your heart.

They blossom radiantly;
lovely buds and blooms
you have given of yourself
to nurture and protect.

When this love has been uprooted,
you till, vigorously, the soil
of your tender heart,
upturning a fresh bed
and leaving no visible trace
of root, stem, or crushed petal
to fall underfoot as you
trudge along determined to rebuild.

New seeds are planted,
and though it is with doubt,
you allow yourself to
tenderly cultivate anew.

However, the perfumed fragrance
of old love will linger long after
the flora has withered.

You cannot completely uproot
everything; every once in a while,
you will find an old flower
has stubbornly clung to its bed
and pushes its way up
among the new rows.

Let these few seeds remain.
Do not uproot everything
simply for the sake of ripping
from the root a small reminder
of your vulnerability and trust.

Instead, cherish the fact that
you allowed yourself to sow
a love so deeply that
a part of it will always remain.

Enjoy this occasional reminder
of beauty and brokenness,
as you grow in new and better ways.

1 Kings 11:41 Now the rest
of the acts of Solomon,
all that he did as well as his wisdom,
are they not written
in the Book of the Acts of Solomon?

If Only

History is much colder
than you ever imagined,
far warmer than you've dreamed,
more dangerous than you ever thought,
less glamorous than we've written it,
and even more boring
than the latest generation sees it.

To be sure, there are many lessons
to be learned from its study;
but we dare not fool ourselves
into believing that the version currently playing
at the Rialto of Memory Lane
is any less a fairy tale than the stories
we read to our grandchildren.

When we see ourselves
as its preservationists,
we would do well to remember
that the thing to which we naturally cling
is mostly a figment of skewed reminiscence;

that our own constitutions
would likely wilt beneath the weight
of its actual ancient burden;
and that its primary purpose
is to give us wisdom and courage
to move forward, not to seduce us,
siren-like, to wistfully turn back.

Hebrews 11:13b They confessed that they were strangers and foreigners on the earth…

Deuteronomy 10:18 He defends the cause of the orphan and the widow, and loves the alien, giving him food and clothing. 19 And you are to love those who are aliens, for you yourselves were aliens in Egypt.

Strangers in a Foreign Land

When Scripture describes us
as "strangers and foreigners on the earth"
we would rather see this
as metaphorical or historical,
not directly applicable to our own situation,

because our simplified, bumper-sticker theologized,
sound-byte-driven culture works best
when we are squeezed into one of two extremes:
either we are IN (on the cozy, privileged inside)
or we are OUT (WAAY out there
on the ostracized and dangerous periphery),
and Lord, you know how hard
we've worked to "make it."

> But there it is, in black & white,
> peppered throughout the Hebrew Scriptures,
> woven into the core of the Greek Scriptures,
> pushing us all up against people
> who wear the labels:
> Illegal Alien, Undocumented Worker.

> Don't get us wrong, Lord.
> We like low-cost produce and cheap labor,
> so long as we don't have to consider
> that its cheapness is inversely related
> to the price these families and individuals pay
> when they are separated and worked
> like mistreated animals in order
> to provide not even their basic necessities.

We're all for border control,
now that our ancestors have long-since
made safe passage from Europe and other ports,
safely ensconced as privileged but anesthetized
citizens of this great and powerful nation.

When we come to worship, O Lord,
we don't mind confessing a little anger,
 a bit of greed, a pinch of lust.
But please don't make us think about
our complicity-via-the-blind-eye
toward complex institutional sin
that has slowly evolved over centuries,
as piecemeal policies have slowly
formed an ever-tightening noose
around us and our economy.

Please don't expect us to consider
giving up the privileges and progress
that we've gained because the playing field
is now tilted like Kilimanjaro's slope.
There. Now we've said it;
named the fear and 'fessed-up the feelings.

Now, speak your truth to us
as we seek to rest in your grace.
Give us wisdom that we may discern
the weed-grown path of strong resistance
winding up the mountainside
of interpersonal relationships,
through the minefield of international politics.

Grant that we may find the courage
to name the sacred cows,
the compassion to speak and act with integrity,
the character to keep going when no one's looking,
 the tenacity to tirelessly trek
all the way to the mountaintop of justice.

Psalm 71:9 Do not cast me off in the time of old age; do not forsake me when my strength is spent.

Age to Age

From age to age we pass
      and though we may look back,
            it's never quite as we remember;
                  neither is forward an easy option.

For the ever-increasing orneriness
      of the elderly in our midst:
            may we be appropriately sympathetic
                  to the new and fearful ground

of ever-deepening loss
      they are daily breaking; and
            may they recognize and acquiesce
                  to the genuine concern and wisdom

with which we hold and care for them.
      Grant patience and persistence
            to those nearest, as they bear
                  the brunt of deep frustration.

Lord, we are not sure which is harder,
      growing old or having to deal
            with those who've beat us to the punch.
                  Regardless, let your grace abound.

Philippians 4:7 And the peace of God, which surpasses all understanding,
will guard your hearts and your minds in Christ Jesus.

Scheduled

Tomorrow is the day, O Lord – big day.
Big because so much of it
is beyond my control.
Big because the closer it gets,
the smaller I feel.

Tomorrow is the day, O God – day of fear.
Fear because I've got no guarantees.
Fear because I haven't been there yet.

Tomorrow is the day, O Lord – "S" word day.
"S" for surgery; "S" for someone else-- I wish.
"S" for surgeon; "S" for safely through-- I hope.

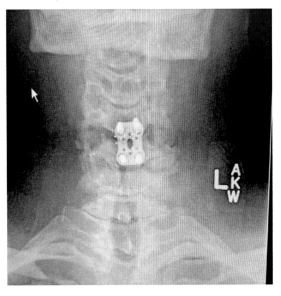

Tonight is the night, O God – longest night.
Long because my mind won't disengage.
Long for the sleep I'm longing for.

Tonight is the night, O Lord – darkest night.
Dark for the unknowing.
Dark for the waiting.

Tomorrow is the day, O God-- your day.
Yours because the knowledge,
skill & wisdom used are
gifts of your graciousness.

Yours because your will
includes love for me and mine.

Tomorrow is the day, O Lord-- your day.
Yours because lilies of the field are clothed.
Yours because hairs are numbered,
and not even a sparrow falls...

Tonight is the night, O God-- your night.
Yours because perfect peace
is a gift of your graciousness.
Yours because true rest
comes only from the depths
of your love.

Tonight is the night, O Lord-- your night.
Yours because the palm
of your hand is big enough.
Yours because the palm
of your hand is loving enough.

I surrender the bigness, the fear,
the "S" word, the longness, and
the darkness to you.
I trust that your graciousness,
love, peace, rest, and the palm
of your hand are enough
to protect me tonight and tomorrow.

Good night, God.
See you in surgery.

Luke 18:16 But Jesus called for them and said, "Let the little children come to me, and do not stop them; for it is to such as these that the kingdom of God belongs. 17 Truly I tell you, whoever does not receive the kingdom of God as a little child will never enter it."

Growing Christmas

If growing-up required you
to shrink from all mystery,
to avoid expectation,
to deny and hide all vulnerability,
jettisoning these child-like qualities
for a strong, planned, and predictable life,
Christmas invites you,
every year, to reclaim its gift.

You will not likely anticipate
the same things you did in your youth,
but you can learn how to wait,
and hope for the arrival
of gift that surpasses imagination.

Christmas invites you
to keep your inner child,
but trade-in your youthful longings
for much larger ones.

When toys and transportation
are no longer at the top of your list,
you have a chance to dream
more amazing gifts.

Hope isn't wishful thinking,
but the realization that the universe
is ordered to point toward a promise
that cannot be denied or derailed.

Peace on earth is not a theory
or an in-breaking for the distant future,
but a courageous act and kind word
chosen each day and moment.

Joy is a gift unwrapped daily,
by those who cease
their own personal pursuit
of happiness long enough
to recognize what's been
underneath the tree all along.

Love is the freely-offered overflow
of those who've traded-in earning
for unconditional grace that shows up
in spite of all our fear and hiding.

Find the child in you so that
you may find the child whose gift
gives us all a chance to be
broken Christs to our hungry world.

*Mark 12:12 When they realized
that he had told this parable
against them, they wanted
to arrest him, but they
feared the crowd.
So they left him and went away.*

Parable

It's a deceptively simple story
spoken at a volume and tone
that are just beyond your
auditory capacity, more at the level
of eavesdropping than conversation.

It leaves the front door cracked,
knowing that you cannot resist peeking
and then sneaking inside to get
a better listening to and look
at what you believe to be an imagined,
but still intriguing tale about
people and places that are
wholly (but not holy) "other."

When the words stop flowing,
if you find yourself gasping in surprise,
both because you didn't realize
you have fully become a character
in the story, and because this took you
all the way to people and places
you'd never approach on your own,

the parable has accomplished its task.
If you completely avoid that breath-taking
experience, you can rest assured you have
escaped unscathed, but perhaps,
not with your life.

2 Samuel 12: 16 David therefore pleaded with God for the child; David fasted, and went in and lay all night on the ground. 17 The elders of his house stood beside him, urging him to rise from the ground; but he would not, nor did he eat food with them.

(Photo by Lee Lindsey McKinney)

Half-Burned Candle

A deeper grief may never be known
than the one that grips you now.
Beyond the next breath and step
is likely too far to see or imagine.

May God's breath be just as close
as the words of those who gather
to hold you firmly along this
fearful, light-starved journey.

May God's compassion never be
farther away than the tears of
those whose words have broken down,
leaving them to give the gift of presence.

May you keep putting one foot
in front of the other until
the shadow of this deep valley
is overcome by the future's glow.

May you find the strength to let God
hold the emotional tsunami that engulfs you;
the courage and wisdom to
grieve your way into the one true hope.

Joel 2:28 Then afterward I will
pour out my spirit on all flesh;
your sons and your daughters
shall prophesy, your old men
shall dream dreams,
and your young men shall see visions.

(Photo by Cyndi Crafton Bagley)

Dreamers

Clouds descend to offer
their cryptic messages
in smoke signal form.

Those who still themselves,
long enough to find
measured breath and peace within,

need no other code
to decipher creation's blueprint.
Listen, and the universe will tell you,

not only the story
of her past, but also
her dreams of our future.

Matthew 16:25 (MSG) Follow me and I'll show you how.
Self-help is no help at all. Self-sacrifice is the way, my way,
to finding yourself, your true self. 26 What kind of deal is it
to get everything you want but lose yourself?
What could you ever trade your soul for?

(Photo by Lee Lindsey McKinney)

In Dependence

Though it may feel like
a courageously climbed mountain,
independence is more
of a slippery slope.

It's not the freedom
to choose what others can't,
not the freedom
to have what others don't.

Each of its manifestations comes
with a price; each release
attaches a sometimes-invisible tether.

Country to country,
economy to economy,
people to people;
no piper goes unpaid.

It's the freedom to be
who others can't:
the one true, connected self
of voluntary gifting and dependence
for which God created you.

There's really only one
freedom that's free –
that doesn't entangle the universe
in a throat-grasping imbalance of desperation.

*Matthew 7:15 "Beware of false prophets, who come to you
in sheep's clothing but inwardly are ravenous wolves.*

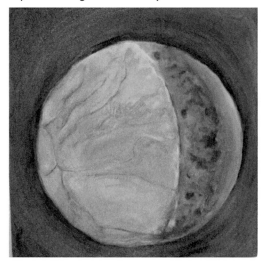

(Self-Portrait of a Damaged Retina, painted by Holly Jenkins Williams)

Blind Ear

What happens when we stereotype
and demonize people who
are different from us,
that we don't know?

What happens when our fear
of them obliterates any perception
of our own individual or corporate
complicity in the chasm between us?

What happens when religion
is indiscriminately bundled
with politics and economics?

Watch the newspaper.
Read the television.
See the radio.
Smell the Internet.
This is what happens.

2 Chronicles 34:31 The king stood in his place and made a covenant before the Lord, to follow the Lord, keeping his commandments, his decrees, and his statutes, with all his heart and all his soul, to perform the words of the covenant that were written in this book. 32 Then he made all who were present in Jerusalem and in Benjamin pledge themselves to it. And the inhabitants of Jerusalem acted according to the covenant of God, the God of their ancestors.

Commitment

I find the Spanish translation of *"commitment"* to be quite revealing regarding our western practice and understanding.

One way to translate it is *obligación*; another is *dedicación*. But when the word is used in a sentence related to something political – for instance, a billboard describing a candidate's commitment to the electorate – the word *compromiso* is used, which is directly connected to the English word "compromise".

Does this mean that the Spanish language recognizes that being committed to something requires the willingness and ability to compromise? If so, this understanding speaks volumes to our current political situation.

When you are committed, to a relationship, a job, a state, or nation, there are certain ways that you must be willing to compromise. No compromise, no commitment. That explains a lot.

Ecclesiastes 9:11 Again I saw that under the sun the
race is not to the swift, nor the battle to the strong, nor
bread to the wise, nor riches to the intelligent, nor favor
to the skillful; but time and chance happen to them all.
12 For no one can anticipate
    the time of disaster.
      Like fish taken
      in a cruel net,
    and like birds caught
      in a snare,
    so mortals are snared
    at a time of calamity,
      when it suddenly
      falls upon them.

(Photo by Jane Hines)

Skin

For all the days when we
are train wrecks with skin on,
O God, we pray for the courage
and patience to let you gently gather
the widely scattered debris,

shift the track ahead with the tender but firm
fire of your Holy Spirit, and redirect
the engine and cargo of our lives toward
a destination of your choosing.

For the few times when our own baggage
happens to have been recently secured,
our own cars uprighted and track-steadied,
give us compassion and courage

to offer all whom you've formed us into
and all with which you have gifted us
toward those whose own flesh
barely contains their current derailment.

Remind us that life is not a race
to the end of the track,
but a many-charactered story

whose mystic healer gave grace away
at every crossing; whose end came,
not when everyone had been convinced
or conquered, but when unconditional love
had been blessed, broken, poured out,

and shared with all who accepted
an invitation to table; invited,
not because of who they were
or what they'd amassed or accomplished,

but because they recognized,
if only for an instant,
the freedom and power
in no longer pretending that their own lives
are a well-deserved, scenic tour of utopia.

Isaiah 55:13 Instead of the thorn shall come up
the cypress; instead of the brier shall come up
the myrtle; and it shall be to the Lord for a memorial,
for an everlasting sign that shall not be cut off.

Memorial

More than never forgetting,
let us always remember,
which is not really the same.

The former, a way
of holding-on to the past,
with no clear avenue to the future;

the latter, a gift for carrying forward,
in hopeful and life-giving ways,
the people and stories who preceded us.

(Photo by Jane Hines)

May we reanimate the lives
of those whose bravery and sacrifice
are foundations for our existence,

with enough consciousness and courage
to differentiate between love for them
and revulsion for what they had to do.

May our memories of those whose lives
were taken by war, in whole or part,
and those whose appearance and affect

Let waving flags and unwavering pride
never swell for the hell of war itself,
but for those who descended into its bowels,

seem to have mostly dodged destruction,
be one part filled with love, respect,
and appreciation for their selfless answer

by force or choice, to face the demons formed
when greed, godlessness, and fear overcome
the common bonds of all humanity.

to duty's call, and another part filled
with the grief of knowing that we must
somehow find a different road to walk.

Let one-eyed squints down loaded barrels
be not consumed by death's insatiable appetite;
praying, instead, to commit the lesser of evils.

Psalm 139:15 My frame was not hidden
from you, when I was being made
in secret, intricately woven
in the depths of the earth.
16 Your eyes beheld
my unformed substance.
In your book were written
all the days that were formed
for me, when none of them
as yet existed.

(Photo by Kathy Chambers)

Painted

Just words, connecting the dots
enough to sketch the big picture;
remembering that, with water color
or crayons or charcoal or even
a bucket of house paint,

however and in whatever shade
your life is decorated today,
the One who dreamed
and drew you before you were born
has your image on the fridge;

your outside-the-lines self
that sometimes feels insignificant
and hurts in ways and places
you'd prefer to have never known.

Never beyond the divine gaze,
your pain and passion,
your hurt and hope
are always on God's heart;
your wholeness being whispered
onto the canvas this instant.

Genesis 32:30 (MSG) Jacob named the place Peniel (God's Face)
because, he said, "I saw God face-to-face and lived to tell the story!"

Obsession

Information is our culture's new drug of choice.
Convinced that more will get us higher
and overdosing is impossible,
we demand ever-larger syringes-full
and smoke it like it's going out of style.

Giddy with increasingly useless varieties,
we no longer care about quality or purpose.
Self-absorbed, we are sots filled only with
the numbing repetition of data
insulating us from reality.

(Photo by Lee Lindsey McKinney)

Our minds and spirits saturated with trash
equivalent to Sterno strained through a loaf of bread,
we're neither capable of connecting
with narratives nor people.

All we can do is spout irrelevance in random patterns,
the synapses of communion long-since atrophied.
So insidious is this hallucinogenic that we
completely fail to appreciate the logical disconnect
between our appetite for it and our paranoia
regarding broad distribution of our personal data.

Deliver us, O Lord, from this addiction
and its accompanying implosion.
Clear our caches that we might once again
store and retrieve sagas of community.
Gather our fragmented bytes that
they might be archived by love.

Show us again the miracle of stillness,
the healing of silence, the grace of space,
that we relearn the art of interfacing
our memoirs with yours and others',
through the unifying gift of our risen storyteller.

Matthew 22:9 Go therefore into the main streets, and invite everyone you find to the wedding banquet.' 10 Those slaves went out into the streets and gathered all whom they found, both good and bad; so the wedding hall was filled with guests.

(Photo by Lee Lindsey McKinney)

Always

Compassion is not fine china
    you pull out on those rare occasions
        when the moon of your generosity
           and the stars of deserving people
                align for an elegant dining experience.

Neither is it a hand extended downward
    in pity, quickly withdrawn to security
        when its precious cargo has been delivered.

It is, instead an everyday,
    moment-by-moment, person-to-person
        way of thinking, speaking, acting, living.
           It is love, not just in action, but also interaction.

Song of Solomon 1:15 Ah, you are beautiful, my love; ah, you are beautiful; your eyes are doves.
16 Ah, you are beautiful, my beloved, truly lovely.

Lover

More of who I am is what I'd like to give you,
not as if the me-ness of it makes it grand,
but because love– desire is its face–
drives me to know as I want to be known;

to risk the whole of who I am
in the comfort of your presence,
trusting you to hold my self-ness
dear and safe with tender care;

to hear, feel, taste ourselves let go
of all that frightens us about
who we are from skin to deepest deep,
reflecting God's gift of unconditionality.

That's my Valentine dream for us,
this day and this remaining lifetime.
Join me if you dare, and make appointment
to live and love and share forevermore.

2 Chronicles 6:19
Regard your servant's prayer
and his plea, O Lord my God,
heeding the cry and the prayer
that your servant prays to you.

(Photo by Jane Hines)

Hurry Up and Wait

"Time is of the essence."
Schedule and plan for treatment carefully
balanced between speed, accuracy;
agreed upon by consulting professionals,
plotted for patient, family, friends to follow.

Operational risk deemed necessary,
surgical trauma's recovery time measured,
monitored; maximum strength, recuperation
desired before next step can follow;
then insurance inserts its monkey wrench.

Hands of the clock, O Lord,
have been spinning out of control since
the first visit's diagnosis erupted
into our lives, shattering all
previous measuring devices.

Time as chronology has become the new enemy,
upping the ante from wrinkles, creaking joints
to an all-in that is beyond our ability to cover;
minutes, hours, days, weeks, months threaten
to become obsessive-compulsive vortex.

Torturously second guessing ourselves,
squeezing all talismans in hopes of going
back in time to replay the scene;
frantically seeking a holy do-over,
begging the clock to cease
its unpredictable palpitations.

Give ear, O God, to swirling chaos;
bring us a new understanding of time—
a measure of holy *kairos*:
clock of your love, grace, plan;
birthing in us the gift of your "right time."

We don't just need pie-in-the-sky
assurance of unimaginable glory beyond
our breathing; give us measuring gifts
for these days, scales by which
to compare our fear and pain
in the balance of your
mercy, forgiveness, wholeness.

Bring us to the place where we can touch
the in-the-flesh promise of Messiah:
one who pitched a tent in our yard,
not as temporary tuxedoed visitor,
but daily companion in the struggle.

Let us synchronize our watches
with the balm of Gilead's tears;
give us a sense of the palpable presence
of the one whose healing flow washes
over all who cry out for help.

Exodus 22:26 If you take your neighbor's cloak in pawn,
you shall restore it before the sun goes down;
27 for it may be your neighbor's only clothing
to use as cover; in what else shall that person sleep?
And if your neighbor cries out to me,
I will listen, for I am compassionate.

Defining Moments

We're sorry if your definitions
of essential and affordable
are different from ours;
if the things you can't provide for yourself
can't be lived without.

You should have thought about that
before you chose to be born into
your family, culture, and socioeconomic class.

Those of us who chose more wisely
can afford to imagine that we don't
need much help at all.

Law is tilted in favor of the haves,
because the more you have,
the more you need;

but there comes a point when we notice
that others are getting things
from government that we already have,
even things we've gotten "on our own".

That's when we opt for politics,
knowing that we'll get to decide
what's in the line and who isn't.

After a while, we begin to believe
that some people aren't really people at all;
that God loves those who can help themselves
and everybody else is just lazy.

As gratitude and humility evaporate,
they leave a hazy crust
of greed and hubris,
through which we can neither
see nor feel our neighbor.

We are left to our own devices,
looking down with contempt,
and up with envy,
skewed beyond recognition
to the universe's parallel nature.

God help us!

Genesis 45:7 God sent me
before you to preserve
for you a remnant
on earth, and to keep alive
for you many survivors.
8 So it was not you
who sent me here, but God;
he has made me a father to Pharaoh,
and lord of all his house
and ruler over all the land of Egypt.

Minimalism

The Future popped-in
again today, re-inviting you
to continue the journey.

She said the road will feel
much less steep if you don't
carry your past the whole way.

The best parts of yesterday
are what make you into
who you are today,
so there's no need to keep
dragging them along.

Continuing to remind others
of them will diminish both you
and today by keeping you
trapped in the past tense.

The worst parts of yesterday
have also impacted your present.
Learn from them and drop them off
at the recycling center.

When others try to drag them up,
politely decline to handle them.
You won't have room for today's gifts
if you keep picking up yesterday's garbage.

*Psalm 119:35 Lead me
in the path
of your commandments,
for I delight in it.
36 Turn my heart
to your decrees,
and not to selfish gain.
37 Turn my eyes from looking
at vanities;
give me life in your ways.*

(Photo by Jennie Roberts Jenkins)

Reveal

Teach us, O Creator of the universe,
to un-hoard our lives
by letting go of the things
we think we need,

so that we can make room
in our homes and hands
to gently cup the beating heart
and fluttering wings of your promise.

Gift us with a peace that nestles us
secured but un-smothered
in a willingness to risk
our whole selves to your providence.

Romans 12:13 Contribute
to the needs of the saints;
extend hospitality to strangers.

Why?

When my options are mine,
not just because of my choices
or my hard work, but also because
of the circumstances of my birth –

the nationality on my passport,
the religion of my ancestors,
and the color of my skin –

and my options aren't yours
for the very same reasons,
how are we to live in this world?

Justice, when he is disentangled
from retribution and violence,
isn't so much about prying privilege
from one hand and placing it in another,

as he is about restoring
creation's balance of need;
about smoothing the universe's supply
of dignity, respect, and opportunity.

If we hope to move beyond
legislated and litigated varieties,
which must be continually replanted,
Justice's sister, Peace,
must be made to feel at home.

Her neighborhood is the place
where stories are shared,
where ears are tilted to understand
and not cocked to respond.

She unpacks Privilege's truth,
inviting us to not only see
our economy of distribution
in all its naked disparity,

but also to choose a life
grounded in a commitment
to be open to and opened by
the question "Why?";

to recognize that it not only
doesn't have to be this way,
we also aren't meant to stay this way.

1 Thessalonians 5:16
Rejoice always,
17 pray without ceasing,
18 give thanks in all
circumstances; for this is
the will of God in Christ
Jesus for you.

Living Prayer

When I realized that all is prayer,
it changed everything,
or at least it changes everything

on those occasions –
more rare than I would like to admit –
when the prayerfulness
of each present moment
does not elude me.

Those careless or caring words
with people who are committed,
by genetics or betrothal,
to spend a lifetime with us?
Prayer.

That erupting criticism or praise
of people whose livelihoods
are purposefully tied to us,
by shared employment
or economic interaction?
Prayer.

Those words never spoken,
because they're never thought,
about the invisible ones
we walk and live right past each day?
Prayer.

That post you shared,
whether or not you envisioned
those with whom it would resonate
or those whose rage it might ignite?
Prayer.

That wishing, both backward and forward,
past regrets and future hopes,
sometimes wholly selfishness
and others, holy selflessness?
Prayer.

Never imagine, then,
that you didn't have/make time for it,
that you didn't do enough of it.
Just try to pay attention to how
you're constantly doing it.
Prayer.

Psalm 84:3 Even the sparrow
finds a home, and the swallow
a nest for herself, where she
may lay her young,
at your altars, O Lord of hosts,
my King and my God.

Unpacking

Grace is not a landfill
 in which we can regularly
  dump the caustic baggage
  of our earthly sojourn;

  neither is it an excuse
   to ignore the consequences
   of our unclaimed freight.

 Rather, it is the promise that,
  once the incarnate bell-hop
   has helped deliver all our luggage –
    be it a neatly matched set,
      or a menagerie of frayed duffels
        and complementary satchels –

   he will help us carefully unpack
      each fragile and frightening item,
        not burying them in the back yard,
          but revealing to us how each piece
            has shaped and formed our temporary residence.

Beyond this safe and complete unpacking,
     we are shown two salvific realities:
       [1] who we have become; and
       [2] the path toward divine plans for our future.

   In these two lie the possibility
       of finally and fully arriving at a place
         that's always been home.

Luke 9:58 And Jesus said to him,
"Foxes have holes,
and
birds of the air have nests;
but the
Son of Man
has nowhere
to lay his head."

(Photo by Owen Todd Jenkins)

Fox Holes

What if there are no atheists
in the paths of tornadoes,
like there are none in war's fox holes;
all of us "praying away",
instead of "praying up" a storm?

    Then, God doesn't have to choose sides
    or conduct evaluations to determine
    whose prayer wins the essay contest,

        and the storm is free to follow
        her own wild and stubborn path,
        like she was going to anyway;
        and we all – survivors, victims,
        and friends alike – can cling
        to the divine promise of presence,

            no one having to believe
            that grace wasn't big enough
            to cover them or their loved ones,
            because it's far larger than that.

Matthew 5:9
Blessed are the
peacemakers,
for they will be called
children of God.

Dance

A rude awakening
from life's peaceful slumber,
death delivers its powerful
kick in the gut,
dancing a victory jig
as we scramble to reorient.

Clamoring for breath
like asthma patients
without rescue inhalers,
we check our lifelines,
jettisoning all lesser gods,
as the truth of their inferiority
becomes apparent.

Dogma and doctrine fade,
as do belief, rules, and rituals.
What's left?

"Hope" may best describe
the place where who we are
and what happens to us along the way
meet the plans and purposes
that God has for us,
both in the here and now
as well as in the hereafter.

Love, the dance that animates us,
when time, distance,
and even breath itself
separate us from those whose hearts
are forever intertwined with ours.

Freedom

It really has no thumbnail view;
won't be found where "me and mine"
live in homogenously gated communities;
bolts unannounced with claustrophobia
when its definition is squeezed
into the privatized closet of self.

Violence and control are temporary.
The forces of the universe can only
be held at bay for so long before
cracks in the dam of possessiveness
begin to leak the world back into balance.

Freedom resides outside the walls,
beyond the cliffs, near the beach,
where the sea of humanity steadily
and gently laps against earth's shore.

That's where the hungry are fed,
the naked clothed, the sick healed,
and the dead laid to rest in peace.

It knows no borders, fears no differences,
sleeps with neither medicine nor anxiety;

is possessed by God and possesses not.

Genesis 3:19
By the sweat of your face
you shall eat bread
until you return
to the ground, for
out of it you were taken;
you are dust,
and to dust
you shall return."

Reflections

When ashes are imposed –
as if we have no choice in the matter –
the only way we can see them
is by reflection.

What do we see, if we pause
to reflect on the oil and ashen stripes
smudged vertically and horizontally
on our foreheads?

Perhaps it may appear as if
it's our cerebral matter peeking,
leaking out, pouring our deepest thoughts,
oft hidden, now exposed
for all the world to see.

> Or maybe it's the dusty grey mess
> of our life's collective catastrophes
> in all their naked embarrassment.

And yes, it surely is a stark reminder
that all of us will go, sooner or later,
back into the earth,
composted toward the future.

But let it also remind us that each of us
contains, in the core of our existence,
a spark of divine hope meant to burn
brightly for all the world to see,

> not because we, ourselves, can muster,
> much less create it, but that Love itself
> has chosen to share this glowing grace
> with us all, and called us to let it burn
> from birth to death, unhindered.

Great Prayer of Thanksgiving
(Living Waters for the World)

When we read your word, O God,
through the sunglasses of our culture,
the pounding percussion we hear
barks these 3 words: I. NEED. MORE!!!
And the economy of scarcity
tightens its grip on us.
We become possessive, like Lot and Abimelech,
arguing with Abraham over wells;
degrading your gifts into commodities, O Lord.

We are too busy to heed Noah's call,
and the flood of too much
of a good thing consumes us.
We become Pharaohs
who order our chariots
to race through the Reed Sea
in pursuit of profit at all costs.
We become emperors and kings
who hoard our bread and wine,
and trade on the hardships of others,
so that we can confiscate
their bread and wine, too, because,
one day there may not be enough.

Ah, but when we let your story
become our story, reading with
open minds, open hearts,
and open dreams, the rhythmic
cadence we hear sounds like these 3 words:
MORE. THAN. ENOUGH.
Then we can pitch our tent
with Abraham and Sara,
setting out for parts unknown,
in the assurance that God will provide.
We are able to follow Miriam and Moses
across dry ground and desert, whining a little,
but glad to partake of water from the rock
and gather our manna every day.

We might even dare to follow Jesus
into the wilderness on a regular basis
to be transformed by silence and
the absence of all the things
on which we have relied,
because we know that there is no place
or people beyond the reach of grace.

In your marvelous ecosystem, O God,
we find elemental
and sacramental providence
in water, bread, and wine.
We find ourselves looking
for opportunities to reflect
and become your hands and feet,
your pipes, pumps, and filters,
in places near and far.

We find ourselves becoming partners
 that give and receive the blessings
of our common humanity,
not as possession or commodity,
but as gift freely offered.

This day, we pray that you would rescue us
from "I need more!" and deliver us
toward "More than enough!" —
that you would keep us
a little hungry and a little thirsty,
so we might better understand the plight
of our sisters and brothers everywhere
who regularly find themselves
at the end of the line and the back of the bus.

This day, as we swallow just a pinch
and a dip of bread and wine,
and as we remember the power
and gift of clean water,
keep us hungry and thirsty for righteousness.

Let us borrow words and strength from
the communion of saints;
let us remember those whose words and deeds
still mirror grace on the path we tread.
Recalling the words spoken
by your prophet Amos and later interpreted
by your servant, Martin, whose ministries
and memory are on our hearts:
let justice roll down,
not like January's cold molasses,
but instead like April's overflowing stream.
Let us be nourished in body, mind, and spirit,
to be your bread and wine in the world,
and to be your conduits of clean water
in all the thirsty places to which you call us.

These and all prayers we offer,
in the name of the incarnate one,
who pitched his tent in our wilderness
and taught us to pray as we join
our hearts and voices together,
praying... Our Father.....

(Photo by Anne Shurley)

2 Samuel 22:5
For the waves of death
encompassed me,
the torrents of perdition
assailed me;
6 the cords of Sheol
entangled me,
the snares of death
confronted me.

Swing Low

For some, the big picture
has been so bright and crisp
for so long that we are lulled
into forgetting its fragility;

and then we are knee-capped
by a storm of epic proportions.
Sure, other storms threatened,
looming darkness on the horizon,
but they are weathered steadfastly.

In one fell swoop, the multi-LED beam
turns into a shadowy flicker,
at risk of being extinguished
by nothing stronger than a gentle breeze.

All these years, abiding in prayer
for others, hoping them toward God
with all the faith we could muster,
trusting beyond our own limits.

Now, the IV's in the other arm,
and we're staring at the ceiling,
surrounded by loved ones.

May the supplications once uttered
from a distance now swing us
into that prayerful hammock,
letting go to the gentle rhythm of grace.

Matthew 13:44
The kingdom of heaven
is like treasure
hidden in a field,
which someone found and hid;
then in his joy
he goes and sells
all that he has
and buys that
field.

Space

Introverts are not nearly
as afraid to speak and hear
as you might imagine.

We do, however,
value words to the point
that more of them will not be added

to a time and place before
the echo of those previously spoken
has faded and their wisdom been absorbed.

So, if you're interested
in knowing our story,
you might elicit its unfolding

by honoring your own tales
with a little more space
than might seem necessary.

Who knows what deeps
we'll find ourselves
treasured into?

(Photo by Jane Hines)

White Bread Jesus

Too much of the work of
the institutional church
feels like feeding white
bread to domestic ducks.

Never mind that its nutritional value
 has been thoroughly denatured
by a bleaching process which
not even God can withstand,

fully oppositional to transfiguration's
amazing glow; or that it doesn't even
stay in our spiritual digestive system
long enough to last us 'til the next meal.

*Revelation 3:15 I know your works;
you are neither cold nor hot. I wish
that you were either cold or hot. 16
So, because you are lukewarm, and
neither cold nor hot, I am about to
spit you out of my mouth. 17 For
you say, 'I am rich, I have
prospered, and I need nothing.'
You do not realize that
you are
wretched, pitiable,
poor, blind, and naked.*

Give us a Jesus that is
palatable and domesticated;
a Savior who goes well with
the rest of our pasteurized lives;
a smoothie, processed
for safe and easy digestion.

God forbid that we should
have to chew and think,
to struggle and be challenged,
to wonder what it means
to be invited to a table

whose menu is "my body,
broken for you" and
"my blood poured out for
the forgiveness of your sins".
No, we'll have White Bread Jesus;
and make that "to go" please.

Teaing

Without denigrating or elevating
two of my favorite beverages,
examine with me, if you will,
what our society does
with them and us.

We are espressoed at every turn,
pitched the idea that speed
is the key to happiness,
and incited to gulp giant java
all day long as productivity's enhancement.

What of life's Oolonging?
Ceremoniously or not,
there is deliberateness and attentiveness
in tea's steeping that awakens us
to life's calming cardiac rhythm.

Shutter speed, it turns out,
is not all it's cracked up to be.
Without attention to focal point,
life is a race to a picture of nowhere.

Psalm 139:15 My frame was not hidden from you, when I was being made in secret, intricately woven in the depths of the earth.

12 Years a Mom
(With Cancer)

It wasn't ever supposed
to happen like this.
Not for anyone.
And yet here we are,
eye witnesses,
ear witnesses, heart witnesses.

Time seems so cruel,
first for its seeming speed,
now for its snail's pace.

And then there's God.

They say the first half of life
is for container-building,
the second half for filling.

Seems like that's all screwed-up here:
all filled-up and no time to share,
all used up and no time to spare.

So now, we hold it all
with sieve-like hands,
watching it pour out,
helpless to do anything
but hope and pray
our way toward you, O God;

helpless without your grace;
becoming more and more aware
that it's not so much
our holding on that matters,
as our being held.

Psalm 63:1 O God, you are my God, I seek you,
my soul thirsts for you;
my flesh faints for you,
as in a dry and weary land
where there is no water.

Ordinary Ministry

We work, play, casually interact
with people every day
who have unspeakable tragedy
lurking just beneath
the surface of their lives.

Sometimes we're on
the other end, finding
tragedy as our own.

Most of the time there's
no longer visible indication
of this suffering;
occasionally- more often than
we probably realize –

thin places show,
where a fresh coat of normal
does not completely hide
what has been buried
in shallow ground.

Stubbing our metaphorical toe
on another's invisible pain;
accidentally raking across
non-sequiturs of
rage, anger, shock.

Momentary silence creates
complete change of subject;
punctuation's pause opens door
to overflowing catacombs of emotion.

Pay attention! These are
places where we can
rise to the occasion
and be fully present;

times for which we are created;
experiences by which,
if we resist the reflex of withdrawal,
we are warmed in love,
soldered together
by God's healing touch;

foundational blocks for
the priesthood of all believers;
blessed sacraments of ordinary ministry.

*Mark 9:24
Immediately
the father
of the child
cried out,
"I believe;
help my
unbelief!"*

(Photo by Jennie Roberts Jenkins)

I Believe

Belief is not something
you defend while you wait
for the world to change or acquiesce.
It's not even something
that changes you.

    It is the intellectual sum
    of the actions you've already taken,
    the questions with which you're wrestling,
    and the relationships you're nurturing.

        When your beliefs stop changing
        and growing, so do you.
        If this happens, no matter what else
        you think you're doing,
        you're mostly just waiting to die.

Acts 10:22 They answered, "Cornelius, a centurion, an upright and God-fearing man, who is well spoken of by the whole Jewish nation, was directed by a holy angel to send for you to come to his house and to hear what you have to say."

Think Again

If you thought you were
bringing Jesus, think again.
Jesus is already where you're going.

If you thought you were
delivering salvific resources, think again.
Creation has provided sufficient stuff
for us all. Maybe you should check
the name tag on some of yours.

If you thought you were
bringing ingenuity and wisdom, think again.
The people who live where you're going
have already figured out
how to do more than
you've ever dreamed, and probably did it
with less than you ever imagined.

If you thought you were
bringing hope, think again.
There's more hope where you're going,
because it's grounded in something greater
than possessions. It's grounded in the great I Am.

Just bring yourself.
That is all.
Yourself and your open mind
and your tender heart.
That is what we need;
what YOU need to show up with.

You bring that, and trust God
to do the rest, and your world
will never be the same again.

Genesis 41:49 So Joseph
stored up grain in
such abundance—
like the sand
of the sea—
that he stopped
measuring it;
it was
beyond measure.

(Photo by Holly Jenkins Williams)

Beyond

Love is a power for others.
If what you have makes you want
a special someone to live and act
in ways that please you,
it is not love.

If what you have makes you feel
warm and tingly, but does not
change the life of someone else
for the better, it is not love.

Love can't be kept to yourself;
it can't exist without making
other people's lives more hopeful,

more meaningful, more joyful.
It overflows to fill

empty places in the universe.

Easter Invitation

Your invitation to this table doesn't arrive in the mail. Neither does mine. It arrived over 2,000 years ago in an upper room, a shared meal, a prayer garden, a love more powerful than death, an empty tomb, and a risen Lord. This is his table, not ours. We are all guests.

When Jesus made his triumphal and final entry into Jerusalem, the people celebrated, waved palm branches, and shouted, "Hosanna!" which means, "Save us now!" If you are hungry for hosanna – for God to feed you with the amazing power of resurrecting love today, and every day – this meal is for you. Welcome home!

A crucial part of the earthly Jesus' transition to risen Christ came at the table on that last night together. Surrounded by those he loved, who were trying to learn how to love, seeking the courage to follow, and desperate to understand, Jesus took bread and wine – the basic elements of human nourishment – and forever connected his presence to them.

He said the bread was his body, breaking and about to be broken for all. We take; we eat; because we are learning that we need to be filled with more than food in order to live and love in the fullness for which God created us. He poured and shared wine, telling them it was his blood in which the sacrifice of love was being written. We take; we drink; because it is becoming increasingly clear that our spirits need quenching as much as our bodies, and love without measure is the only cup that satisfies. And then they went to the garden to pray.

7:49 PM

Aaaand the retreat begins.
First there must be
a withdrawal from all
to which I have become
accustomed and addicted, including:

- responding to others' needs
- writing to speak to those needs
- sucking worth out of their responses

There's a crow in a tree
about 100 feet from the front window.
He's been calling for the past hour,
as I finished some work.

As soon as I settled,
he stopped. I'm pretty sure
that's God, patiently, plaintively cawing.

Now I hear the dogs (coyotes?)
begin their sunset song.
But only for a few minutes.
Then a sacred silence floats in.

The trees dance their green at me,
as the wind pulses its ever-erratic rhythm
through their nimble extremities.

The sky's once-dense rain-fog
returns to a steamy afternoon blue,
only to succumb to dusk's pink ribbons.

As the colors fade into evening's gray,
the lightning bugs begin their survival-flash,
conjuring progeny into the fading light.

All through the dimming,
I hear the wind say – for the first time
since I-don't-know-when –

"I sing this song for you every day,
not for you to YouTube it
for someone else, but for your pleasure;

for no other purpose than
your soaking-up the unconditionality
of my grace poured
into evening's sky for pure joy."

Surely but steadily, all of the ego
and pettiness with which my world
has been surrounded begin
to fade with the sun's sinking.

The stillness of holy darkness
gently blows her peace
through the open screens.

I know that I could breathe
like this forever.
Maybe I will.

Call to Scripture

[Leader] *Scripture is the place*
where well-dressed,
comfortable people turn
to have their lifestyles validated.

[People] **No! Scripture**
is the story around which
all people gather
to hear about the lifestyle
God intends for them to live.

[Leader] *Scripture is the place*
for good people to learn
how to become even better.

(Photo by Kendall Cox)

[People] **No! Scripture is the place**
for all people to confess their own sin
and to hear and share
God's good news of forgiveness.

[Leader] *Scripture is the place*
where people go to ask God
for the things they want.

[People] **No! Scripture is the place**
where people offer
what they have received
for the work that God is planning.

[All] *Let us gather to hear scripture,*
that we might learn God's lifestyle,
share God's forgiveness,
and offer ourselves
to God's work.

1 Corinthians 4:21
What would you
prefer? Am I to
come to you with a
stick, or with love in
a spirit of
gentleness?

LML

Seek ye first to be and then to find
a **L**ow **M**aintenance **L**over:
someone who recognizes their own
broken needs for and expressions of love
as the wonderful imperfections they are;

      someone who gives love,
      not for reciprocation,
      but for the sheer joy of catching glimpses
      of how even broken-to-broken
      expressions of it are capable
      of calling forth the joyous
      divine purposes hidden
      deep within us all;

            someone who often realizes
            that sharing intimacy in all its
            glorious manifestations is far closer
            to *imago dei* than reproduction could ever be.

*Luke 23:42 Then he said, "Jesus,
remember me when you come into your kingdom."*

Remember Me

Criminals to the left and right,
Jesus was crucified front-and-center,
as if he somehow might escape
if not completely surrounded.

Mercy was his plea, as the economics
of death played out; soldiers gambling
for the clothes he would never need again:
"Father, forgive them;
they don't know what they are doing."

From one side or the other,
hoping against the crowd's disbelief,
one thief's anger unfurls,
raising the flag of criminal camaraderie,
begging for and yet demanding
deliverance by association, sans contrition.

From the other side, with no leg
but honesty to stand on,
another thief's plea for mercy pours:
"Jesus, remember me when you
come into your kingdom."

"Remember me..." he begs,
as if he knows how powerful a weapon
memory can be against the army of coercion;
as if he already understands how foundational
it is for faith: "This do in remembrance of me."

Silence to the first thief, as if he might still
have an opportunity to respond differently;
hope and promise to the second:
"Truly I tell you, today you will
be with me in Paradise."
Our king; our promise.
Thanks be to God!

Proverbs 25:25
Like cold water to a thirsty soul,
so is good news from a
far country.

Mission

It begins when we listen for God
at work in places
completely foreign to us.

These locations might be
right outside our door,
at a time of day different from
the ones we normally venture out.

They may be across town,
in places we wouldn't travel on purpose,
or across the globe,
in places that, by our own ignorance,
strike fear into our hearts.

God will not fit in a pocket
or a suitcase; needs neither
to be delivered to nor
rescued from any place.

God simply needs to be found.
When we arrive at any place
that is not home -
and perhaps often at home, too -
our initial task should be
to discern all of the ways and
places in which God is already laboring.

Until we do that, and find
the humility to offer the fullness
of ourselves to that which God
is already doing and desires,
mission will completely elude us.

*Matthew 2:12 And having been warned
in a dream not to return to Herod,
they left for their own country
by another road.*

Secrets

Some of them are merely
wrapping paper for surprise,
temporarily covering reality
until the planned moment of joy:
that first pony or puppy,
the weekend getaway to paradise
with one(s) dearly loved.

Others are shadows
marinated in more pain
than seems humanly possible
to bear; bruises and cuts –
maybe even amputations –
that have effected
self-ectomies beyond recognition.

(Photo by Anne Shurley)

Live tenderly with those
who eschew the former.
You never know who
has walked through
the inferno of the latter.

The invitation to trust
cannot be accepted at gunpoint.

Before we can risk wading
into the river of grace,
we must learn to trust
that someone else is holding
onto our brokenness
with the buoy of love
and without the anchor of judgment.

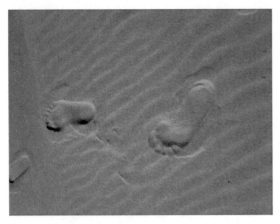

Luke 6:37 Do not judge,
and you will not be judged;
do not condemn,
and you will not be condemned.
Forgive,
and you will be forgiven;
38 give, and it will be given to you.
A good measure,
pressed down, shaken together,
running over, will be put into your lap;
for the measure you give
will be the measure you get back.

When I'm Gone

The older I get, the more I feel
    the angel of death approaching.
        It's rarely a frightening thing;
            more like preparation for the visit
    of a long lost friend, whose arrival time
has yet to be determined.

I am surely saddened by the approach,
    but not because I am concerned
        about what will happen or where I'll go.
            Though evidence and information
    are in short supply, I've let go of worry
and placed my hope firmly in grace.

My sadness stems mostly from the things
    I wish I'd said and done and the ones I'll miss most;
        those whose love coursed powerfully through
            my veins with each breath and heartbeat;
        those whose presence gave my life
meaning, vision, purpose, and passion.

So when I'm gone, I beg of you,
    do these things early and often:
        remember the ways I failed to love and live
            with abandon, respect, and tenderness,
        and set your heart, mind, and spirit
to avoid repeating my mistakes in your life;

remember the ways and times that I,
     by accident and occasionally on purpose,
          stood back far and long enough from self
        to allow God's love to reflect from eye to soul;
     set your heart, mind, and spirit
to reflect more of these graces in your life.

Resolve today, and every day that follows
     to practice the four Ls:
        laugh, love, learn, and live
          as one who more and more understands
        that fear is our biggest waste of time and energy;
     that the math for everything that matters
is abundance: giving more = having more.

Make it part of your life's purpose
     to use things and love people
        and not the other way around,
          for these are the illogical, crazy ways
        of the God who pitched tent among us,
     offering love before forgiveness is requested.

These are things I believe
     are keys to every life's meaning;
        things that will serve you long and well
          as you journey toward the place and time
        where you'll make your own crossover
joining the chorus of the great beyond.

Just in case you're wondering
     what I expect to find on the other side;
        whatever else happens, I expect to say:
          "Wow! This is what it's like to completely love
        and be loved." One day I'll show you!

Scripture Index

Index #2

This is an index of last resort. We hope you'll read all of the entries at least once before you consult this index, and would be perfectly happy if you never used it at all. Why? Because any categorizing of poems/prayers runs the risk of limiting the way they are interpreted. That said, there may be times and circumstances when some sort of ordering may have value. To that end, the entries have been divided into the following five genres: Culturally Prophetic, Ecclesially Prophetic, Generally Pastoral, Specifically Pastoral, and Worship Resources.

Culturally Prophetic
(hopeful imagining for culture at large)

Ecclesially Prophetic
(prayerful dreams for institutional religion)

Ecclesially Prophetic
(continued)

Generally Pastoral
(reminders of the big picture of grace)

Specifically Pastoral
(prayers in the midst of personal life-chaos)

Worship Resources
(litanies, prayers, and other words
for use in corporate worship)

Made in the USA
Middletown, DE
27 March 2015